D0558786

VIETNAM

A LEGACY OF
LONGSUFFERING

The **Voice**
of the **Martyrs**

with Renee Dylan

Living Sacrifice Book Company
Bartlesville, OK 74005

Vietnam: A Legacy of Longsuffering

Living Sacrifice Book Company

P.O. Box 2273

Bartlesville, OK 74005-2273

ISBN 978-0-88264-035-8

Edited by Lynn Copeland

Cover design by Lookout Design

Cover creation, page design, and layout by Genesis Group

Printed in the United States of America

Unless otherwise indicated, Scripture references are from the *New King James* version, © 1979, 1980, 1982 by Thomas Nelson Inc., Publishers, Nashville, Tennessee.

About the cover: Communist propaganda on the streets of Ho Chi Minh City.

VIETNAM

"God has strengthened and helped us. So we keep hoping in Him and fixing our eyes on Jesus. We follow Him to endure the cross, scorning its shame to the point of death."

—PASTOR NGUYEN LAP MA,
arrested for refusing to surrender his
church building to the Communists

*"This is my comfort in my affliction,
for Your word has given me life."*

—PSALM 119:50

VIETNAM

CONTENTS

ACKNOWLEDGMENTS

I am deeply grateful to the many people who supported the writing of this book.

Thank you, Riley K. Smith, for your attentive editing at every stage. I am also thankful for the research you contributed to highlight the oppression facing Vietnam's modern-day Christians.

VOM-Australia staff, thank you for the stories you contributed. It is a joy to collaborate with fellow Christians who are able to so powerfully share the experiences of those suffering for Christ's sake.

Lynn Copeland, I so appreciate your invaluable editing work, which enhanced the clarity and cohesion of this book. Several other VOM-USA staff also played an important role in providing resources and coordination for this project. So my additional gratitude goes to Lynn, Tim, and Carol.

I am also grateful to my friend and fellow *Restricted Nations* series writer Michelle Waters for her support, wisdom, and encouragement along the way.

Finally, I am thankful for the Vietnamese Christians whose courageous testimonies deserve to live on throughout the ages. Their examples of faithful sacrifice and perseverance have challenged me to recognize God's graciousness at work amid adversity.

Reader, I have every confidence that their testimonies will also deeply impact you as you serve our Lord. Thank you for taking the time to read them. I pray that this book not only heightens your compassion for the persecuted, but also assures you that God is indeed victorious. May it compel you to stand with these faithful men, women, and children. Their lives of obedience are but pages in the story of redemption in which you share.

And Lord, I thank you for your unfailing grace—to me, and to us all.

RENEE DYLAN

INTRODUCTION:
A LONG OBEDIENCE

Centuries ago, when Vietnam was known as Annam and was ruled by kings and lords, Christianity was branded a "false religion." Its followers were executed and tortured at the whim of those in power. Some of their bodies were not even given a proper burial but were callously cast into the sea. To disobey those in power in favor of Jesus Christ was to forsake the king and at times their religion, culture, and family—and many paid with their very lives.

This is the Vietnam of years long past, but it is also the Vietnam of today. This hard road of faithful obedience is still being walked by Vietnamese Christians who serve God above all else. There may not be beheadings in the streets, dynastic ascensions to power, or new laws given by edicts and decrees, but the landscape of longsuffering is still the same. Believers are deemed "disloyal" for simply sharing God's Word or gathering to worship Him. They can be beaten, imprisoned, drugged, and even killed for turning their backs on their particular religion. Vietnamese Christians receive little mercy from the world. Theirs is a reality shaped by repressed rights and contested beliefs—just as the days of those who came before them were fraught with injustice and oppression.

Throughout the history of the Vietnamese church, the method of securing mercy from a persecutor has remained the same: deny Christ and renounce faith in Him. This was not the path taken by the faithful. We know because the church was not snuffed out—it persisted, and even grew.

Again and again, obedience to Christ was chosen over loyalty to man. Again and again, an environment of oppression proved to be fertile ground for ministry opportunity. Amid even the most savage of trials, the people of Vietnam refused to give up the truth of salvation through Jesus Christ.

This is the way of the cross walked throughout Vietnam's history, and this is the way of the cross being walked right now, this minute, in the easternmost country on Southeast Asia's Indochina Peninsula. Who are these men and women, these committed and courageous followers of Jesus of past and of present? What can their stories of costly faith tell us about the call Christ has placed on His followers? And how can we embrace the inheritance of hope God has given to us through the Vietnamese church, even in seasons of tears, violence, and loss?

The answers to such questions can be found only by walking alongside the very believers whose lives have inspired them. This book is but one way to take the journey—to witness the trials and victories of God's people in Vietnam. It is a road of bloodshed, but also of blessing; of challenge, but also of comfort. Above all, it is a road of long and loving obedience to God and an invitation to encounter the great mercy granted to all those who suffer for the Lord's sake.

VIETNAM'S FIRST CHRISTIANS (16ᵀᴴ-17ᵀᴴ CENTURIES)

The sixteenth and seventeenth centuries were turbulent times for those who swore allegiance to Christ in Vietnam. After many years of relative calm and acceptance, the church saw an intensification of persecution, including torture and the first known Christian martyrdom in Vietnam. Through it all, they would deepen the witness of Christianity in Vietnam, proving its diversity and vitality, and that it was not just "the religion of the Portuguese." They also testified to the justice of a God who is faithful to those who obey Him—an inheritance of faithfulness drawn on by Christians in centuries to come.

The first recorded evidence of Christianity in Vietnam (then known as Annam, as named by the Chinese in 1164) reveals that it was already facing resistance and scrutiny from those who did not recognize it as the truth. A 1533 edict calls Christianity "the false doctrine of [Jesus]" and prohibits it from being preached in northern villages. The edict specifically accuses a "man from the sea" named "I Nu Khu" (possibility a form of the name Ignatius) of preaching this "false doctrine." The man appears to have been a church leader sailing along the coast and stopping at Vietnam. There is also evidence of Portuguese and Spanish friars undertaking ministry efforts in the late 1600s.

The language barrier kept these initial efforts from producing lasting results, and so it was not until the seventeenth century that the Christian faith would truly become established. Key to this mission of spreading the seed of the gospel in Vietnam was a Jesuit leader who was called "the father of the Christians" in Vietnam. Not only did he have knowledge of the language of the Vietnamese people, he also had a zealous love for bringing them the saving knowledge of Christ and a spirit willing to suffer for the sake of the Father.

The Jesuits Arrive
When the Jesuits arrived in Vietnam in 1615, the country was caught up in a war between the north and south (Tonkin and Cochinchina)—a power struggle fought by rival ruling families, the Nguyen clan and the Trinh clan. The Jesuits arrived in response to a request by the captain of a Portuguese merchant ship to set up a mission in the city of Fai Fo, a growing trading post. Among the Jesuit leaders to arrive shortly after the mission's establishment was a man named Alexander de Rhodes —who would cultivate a legacy of faithful and brave ministry.

It had not been de Rhodes's lifelong plan to serve in Vietnam. Born in Avignon, France, in

1593 and educated in various Jesuit schools, de Rhodes was granted permission to minister in Japan in 1618. However, due to hostility toward Christianity in Japan, his superiors instead sent him to Vietnam, where he arrived in 1619.

When de Rhodes came to Vietnam, he found three main religions: Buddhism, Confucianism, and Taoism. Most of those he encountered viewed Christianity as a purely Portuguese religion; the arrival of Jesuits on Portuguese boats confirmed this view. This association caused both the Trinh and Nguyen leaders to be tolerant of Jesuit missionary presence, and even allowed evangelism, at first, as they believed these foreigners might help them secure trade with Europeans. Christianity was referred to by the rulers, and other Vietnamese, as "the way of the Portuguese" and

Alexander de Rhodes

de Rhodes himself was called "the father of the Portuguese" or "the father of Christians." His ministry, however, would come to testify to the wide claim of the Christian faith—that it was not the way of any one people, but was a path given by the sovereign Lord to all people.

De Rhodes's Mission in Tonkin (1627–1630)

In March 1627, de Rhodes went to Tonkin in northern Vietnam and began a mission that would not only generate much growth for the church, but also serve as a preview of the trials the faithful would face at the hands of the ruling lords.

Christianity had come to Vietnam in relative peace. But when Vietnamese people began to turn to Christianity through de Rhodes's efforts, trouble began. The conversions angered Buddhist monks, as Buddhism was a dominant religion and had been in the country since the second century. They also angered concubines whose men had abandoned them after embracing Christianity.

The bitter Buddhist monks eventually organized a religious debate with de Rhodes, who recruited his fellow missionary Ignatius, a young man with profound knowledge of the Chinese religious books at the root of the monks' beliefs. De Rhodes shared with them about the justice of God—His faithfulness to the obedient and His power against those who opposed Him—using the biblical account of the ever-faithful Shadrach, Meshach, and Abednego as an example. The monks only grew angrier, and accused de Rhodes and his followers of joining a plot against Trinh Trang, the ruling lord. Lord Trang responded by issuing a decree threatening death to those who had contact with the missionaries or who accepted their faith.

After the decree, all missionaries were isolated. They were put under virtual house arrest yet able to communicate with other believers—including de Rhodes, but only through letters. Vietnamese believers decided to organize their own meetings and take up the mantle in a new, more independent way. They would lead prayer and worship services on their own, often incorporating readings of the missionaries' letters. This display of leadership was no doubt welcomed by de Rhodes when he heard of it, as he had a passionate belief that the church in Vietnam would be strongest if built by its own people—not simply by the efforts of outsiders.

During this time Lord Trang gave de Rhodes and Ignatius more freedom, hoping their presence would promote trade with the Portuguese. But eventually they too fell out of favor.

In May 1630, de Rhodes was expelled from the country. While he was never to see Tonkin again, he had not seen Vietnam for the last time.

Persecution in the Land of the Nguyen Lords

After his exile from Vietnam, de Rhodes spent ten years in Macau, China, where he taught theology. Vietnam remained close to his heart, however. In 1639, news came of persecution against Christians in regions ruled by the Nguyen clan. Lord Nguyen Phuoc Lan had ordered seven Jesuits to leave the country after suspecting them of aiding his brother in an attempted coup.

In 1640, de Rhodes would return to Cochin-china, beginning a five-year mission that would prove even more challenging than his ventures in Tonkin. Both he and his fellow workers would face great difficulties for their faith, including exile, violence, and condemnation to death. Three would pay a particularly costly price for their faith: their very lives.

The first of de Rhodes's followers to perish at the hands of the Nguyen lords was Andrew of Phu Yen in July 1644. A young student of de Rhodes, Andrew was kidnapped upon the orders of Lord Nguyen Phuoc Lan, who was disturbed by the number of his soldiers coming to Christ. Andrew was tried by a Vietnamese leader and eventually decapitated after refusing to renounce Christianity. He is considered Vietnam's first known martyr.

In the months following Andrew's death, the persecution intensified in the south of Vietnam. De Rhodes and Ignatius were arrested and questioned about their preaching, and were again ordered to leave the country. However, they chose to defy the order and remain—Ignatius going to the southern provinces and de Rhodes to the northern provinces. Those seeking to drive Christianity out of Vietnam routinely tortured foreign missionaries and new converts, men and women. By daylight, de Rhodes and his workers would often stay low —remaining inside and out of sight—and then work tirelessly by night among the people.

And there were more martyrdoms to come. In 1644, de Rhodes and Ignatius were arrested by authorities while celebrating Christmas. They were soon charged with preaching without the permission of the king. The two men were eventually released, but Ignatius was arrested again a few months later, along with at least two other followers of de Rhodes. They were tried in the court of Lord Nguyen Phuoc Lan, and told they would be released if they renounced their religion. But the men bravely refused to forsake their faith.

De Rhodes would also meet arrest once more, after being apprehended on a ship en route to the city of Fai Fo. He was taken into custody, imprisoned, and condemned to death by the king's court. Just when it seemed the bold leader, teacher, and missionary might meet his end, one of the king's former teachers convinced him that de Rhodes had not committed a crime by preaching. His sentence was then commuted to exile. De Rhodes left the country on July 3, 1645, aboard a Portuguese ship.

Just three days later, the deadly sentences against Ignatius and his fellow partners in ministry were carried out. It was but a year after Vietnam's first known martyr, and already the country's list of martyrdoms was growing. Its people were persevering in the faith, paying the ultimate price, and proving that their love for Christ surpassed all else.

This time, de Rhodes had indeed had his last view of Vietnam. But this "father of Christians" would not forget the people—or they him. His legacy was a lasting one. By the time of his death in 1660 (in Persia), it was estimated that some 6,700 Vietnamese had come to Christ due to the efforts of de Rhodes and his fellow missionaries.

But the impact of de Rhodes's Jesuit mission is certainly not a matter of numbers; it is a legacy of faithfulness not to the lords of the earth, but to the true Lord of all. He had shown that commitment to Christ was not just "the way of the Portuguese," nor even just the way of the Jesuits or the Vietnamese. He demonstrated that Christ's call to repentance and faith was for people of all nationalities—for the young and the old, for men and for women. Such obedience to the Great Commission led to the birth and growth of a Vietnamese church that dared to live and walk in the way of the cross.

WITH PRAYERS
AND TEARS

The police came with guns. It was the late 1970s, just after the Communist takeover, and authorities were scouring Vietnam for church properties to confiscate. In the southern city of Can Tho, Pastor Lap Ma and his family were in charge of a church, and had been appointed to stay there by the Christian and Missionary Alliance.

When police reached the church building, they demanded that the pastor hand over the property to them.

"I am only the manager, not the owner," was Pastor Lap Ma's response. "I will not hand over God's property. If you want to take it, you must sign a paper from a Higher Authority."

"Then we'll shoot you," the officers threatened.

For the "crime" of refusing to relinquish the church property to the Communist Party, Pastor Lap Ma, his wife, and their ten children were placed under house arrest in a tiny, rural village in 1982. All of their possessions were taken and they could travel no more than three kilometers (about two miles) out of the area. The isolation was a kind of prison. For twelve years they had no mail access —another way to cut them off from the outside world.

When at long last authorities loosened the mail restrictions, Pastor Lap Ma was thrilled to see more than three thousand letters arrive at his home! The Voice of the Martyrs had published Pastor Lap Ma's story and his address, and students, housewives, pastors, and businessmen wrote letters of encouragement to the pastor and his family. Vietnamese police were aghast at the support this family received.

Pastor Lap Ma and his family found great strength and encouragement in the letters. To the family, they were not just evidence of the love of their brothers and sisters in Christ, but of the enduring love of their Lord.

The Lap Mas

"I read these letters with prayers and tears," Pastor Lap Ma said, "because I know our Father never will leave us nor forsake us. He has strengthened and helped us."

Pastor Lap Ma and his family would see the outside world again. With help from the U.S. government, they were eventually released from house arrest. Although the government had thought locking up him and his family would stop the spread of the gospel, ten additional churches were planted as a result of his ministry—led by people he helped bring to faith in Christ. Pastor Lap Ma is now retired and living in the U.S., and his children are carrying on the work; nine of them are currently pastors in Vietnam.

"While we are living, God uses us to comfort the other suffering Christians," said Pastor Lap Ma.

May this communion of comfort continue to be lived not just by this family, but by the family of Christ in Vietnam and the borders beyond, knowing that "those who sow in tears shall reap in joy" (Psalm 126:5).

"THE GREAT PERSECUTION": THE RULE OF MINH MANG (19TH CENTURY)

Countless bodies were broken, much blood spilled, and many lives lost during the reign of Nguyen ruler Minh Mang (1820–1841). He and his enforcers sought to make a spectacle of torture, hacking off the limbs of Christians, tearing their flesh with hot tongs, and enslaving them with drugs. At the height of this bloodshed, during a period of but seven years, over one hundred and thirty church leaders, missionaries, and other believers were executed. The repression was so intense that mission records refer to this period as "the great persecution."

His atrocious reign would bring some of the most remarkable testimonies of obedience to Christ in the face of ruthless violence in Vietnam's history. *That* would be the spectacle—the enduring testimony beyond the torture (1 Corinthians 4:9).

Minh Mang's father, Gia Long, had been cautious but tolerant of the church during his reign (1802–1820). While he did not ban or drive out Christians, he did monitor their religious activities closely. But the tolerance the church had known in Gia Long's day shifted swiftly to savagery when his son rose to power.

At the beginning of Minh Mang's rule, it appeared that he might rule like his father and extend a guarded acceptance of the church in Vietnam. In 1825, however, he issued official instructions banning the arrival of new missionaries and ordering all those in the country to gather in one place. It was a warning sign—a clear tactic to isolate and cut off Christian missions at their root—and similar directions would be repeated in 1826 and 1830. In 1833 and 1836, he issued edicts that condemned Christianity, painting it as being in direct and dangerous opposition to the country's social harmony, ancestral history, and Confucianism.

These documents described the religion of the missionaries as a "perverse" belief system that "mesmerizes" its followers into refusal to recant. They also condemned Christianity's teachings about the existence of heaven and hell and refusal to worship Buddha and ancestors.

To the Christians who were standing firm despite pressure to abandon their faith, such rhetoric was an attempt to diminish their testimonies by implying they were merely "brainwashed." The edicts also revealed Minh Mang's intent to mobilize his people to rid the country of Christians for the sake of social "harmony." He was successful in recruiting followers willing to carry out this mission, and raids on Christian communities became commonplace.

Minh Mang's efforts to force new converts to recant intensified in 1836. Until then, village heads had only to submit statements to local authorities documenting those who had recanted. But that year officials began to visit villages and demand that converts line up, one by one, and walk over a cross in order to renounce Christ. If a missionary or even an object representing Christianity was discovered in the community, families or even entire villages could face severe punishment—from exile to torture.

In 1838, two Christian soldiers living in the Red River Delta city of Nam Dinh bravely refused to walk over a cross and recant their faith during a search of their community. The men, Pham Viet Huy and Bui Duc The, refused, claiming that their loyalty to Christ was a matter of filial piety because their ancestors were also allegedly Christians. (By this time Christianity had been in the region for nearly eight generations, so it is indeed possible that these men were born into Christian families.)

In a written account of their refusal, Pham Viet Huy and Bui Duc The state their belief that "faithfulness and filial piety are two fundamental principles of human society." This claim only intensified Minh Mang's view that Christianity disrupted the historical order of family and tradition. It angered not just Minh Mang but his court, which refused their protest and issued a brutal order: several of their fellow soldiers were commanded to physically pull the two men over a cross to enforce their "renunciation." After this was done, both men were released and offered financial reward, which they refused. They traveled to Hue province to appeal to higher authorities. But their attempt at mediation was rejected by the Board of Punishments. The two were instead arrested.

Months later, Minh Mang approved an edict to prevent his people from claiming "filial piety" as a defense for their Christian faith. A short time later Pham Viet Huy and Bui Duc The were executed for refusing to leave "the religion of Jesus." As a kind of brutal warning to other believers, their corpses were cut in half and thrown into the sea.

During this time, Minh Mang also secured the capture of Christians by promising riches and promotions to those who delivered a missionary. However, some Christians, including European missionaries, were able to evade capture due to the fear local mandarins (bureaucrats) had of being punished for failing to report them in a timely manner. For example, even if the location of a new French missionary became known, it might go unreported and the village unsearched because the mandarin responsible feared he could be executed for not reporting the missionary's initial arrival.

Joseph Marchand, a French missionary in Vietnam and member of the Paris Foreign Missions Society, took matters into his own hands in resisting Minh Mang's brutal reign. He later paid with his life. In 1833, he joined forces with the son of a southern Vietnamese official, and together they tried to overthrow Minh Mang and place Minh Mang's Christian nephew on the throne. After two years of working with others in this attempt, Marchand was arrested in Saigon after his involvement in the plot was discovered. There he was put to death, forced to suffer one of the most brutal execution methods of the time: having his flesh pulled off by metal tongs.

The legacy of "the great persecution" of the church in the early nineteenth century lies not in the extent of the torture or death, but in the greatness of Christ and His grace. When Minh Mang died of natural causes in 1841, his rule was over, the brief flame of his earthly life extinguished. Minh Mang could not conquer the church in Vietnam. The Body of Christ he had fought so hard to destroy was still standing—small and scattered, but alive. God was still at work in Vietnam, guiding all of His people and preparing them for the time ahead, whether it bring repression, peace, or revival.

CARRYING THE BURDEN
WITH COURAGE

Young "Tuan" (not his real name) had a long trip ahead. The police had called him in for interrogation, and it was a two-hour hike through the mountain trails from his North Vietnam village to the station. Tuan knew why he was being targeted: his bold work in sharing the Word of God with fellow members of the Dao tribe.

It had been at least three decades since the 1970s Communist takeover of Vietnam. But in Tuan's country, the government still looked at Christianity with great disdain. All Christian literature in Dao, the language of the ethnic group to which he belonged, were illegal. Yet this normally shy teenager was one of many ethnic believers tirelessly committed to sharing Christ with his fellow countrymen, even at great risk to himself. "I know the importance of having the Word of God," he said.

This time, he had come to the attention of the authorities after bringing ten New Testaments and twenty-two hymnbooks in the Dao language to local believers. Three days after the resources were delivered, the police somehow gathered evidence about Tuan's involvement and they called him to the station.

For three days, the police interrogated Tuan. They demanded to know where this boy had gotten the money to travel to get the books.

"I sold my buffalo," he replied. This was a large sacrifice for Tuan, because the buffalo was one of his main means of supporting himself. Still, he gave it up so he could bring Christian literature to those who were hungry for spiritual nourishment.

"Why did you bring a lot of books to this village?" they asked.

"The believers need the books so they can understand what they believe," said Tuan.

The policemen wanted to know whether this boy would dare to continue in this path of disobeying the law. One officer grabbed him by the collar, shouting, "Will you go again to the city to get books?"

"If the officers confiscate all our books, when I have money I will go again," Tuan replied.

"Why don't you obey the government?" the angry policeman asked.

"I trust my Lord," said Tuan. "I will never reject Him. I need the books so I can understand Him."

Tuan returned home, but the police continued to watch him.

Two years later, in August 2007, Tuan was taking the long walk to his village from the main road when police stopped him. They searched his bag, and found on him thirteen hymnbooks, four New Testaments, and four DVDs about Jesus' life. They then forced him to come to the police station.

Once at the station, eight other officers from another district arrived. Officials began to beat Tuan, shouting, "Call your Lord to save you now! Why do you trust in your Lord? When I hit you, you still feel the pain, don't you?" They repeatedly struck his now-bloodied face, and pummeled him in the stomach. He eventually fainted from the blows.

Around 2:00 in the morning, Tuan regained consciousness. But he was not alone—the police were standing around him, watching him. They released him to go home, but demanded that he return to the station the following day.

Tuan left, so sore from his assault that he could not bear to even bend over.

The next day he arrived again at the station.

"Will you still bring back books?" the police asked him again.

"If the officer confiscates these books again, when I have a chance I will go again," said Tuan.

The authorities then fined him and put him under house arrest for three months. Every month he was ordered to report to the village police station. Such trials and scrutiny could be enough to frighten a believer of any age. But they did not

Many Christians travel a long way to share the message of Christ.

stop sixteen-year-old Tuan in his Christian work. He came to be the pastor of a church with forty members. He now takes part in training sessions with Christian leaders who come from rural regions all over the country. Sometimes they meet for many hours in an upstairs room, where it is often hot and stuffy, studying Scripture and receiving biblical training.

To get Christian books, Tuan walks for hours to the main road before taking a twelve-hour bus ride to the city. He rides a bike between villages to minister to believers.

"When I go out, I carry no bag, and I go after dark," says Tuan. "I praise the Lord who protects me."

Pray for young believers like Tuan who risk all for the sake of the gospel. Pray for their safety, courage, and endurance of faith.

VIOLENCE AND GROWTH: THE CHURCH UNDER TU DUC (MID-LATE 1800s)

By the mid-nineteenth century Minh Mang was dead, his reign of "great persecution" ended. His son, Thieu Tri, banned all foreign missionaries from the country, and eventually attempted to imprison those he found. However, he did not demonstrate the same violent hostility as his father against the faith itself, nor did he officially outlaw Christianity during his rule. Some Christians no doubt saw him as lenient compared to the vicious rulers of the past.

When Thieu Tri's son, Tu Duc, took the throne, all Christians imprisoned for their faith were mysteriously pardoned. Many must have been hopeful that the horrific level of violence against Christians was receding. But it was under this man, who came to power at the age of seventeen, that the church in Vietnam would endure a long, intense saga of unimaginable bloodshed.

Much of Tu Duc's escalating aggression toward Christianity over his thirty-six-year reign was shaped by the political battle for control in his time, particularly due to the invasion of Vietnam by France in 1857. His treatment of Christians shifted depending on how he viewed their threat to his dominion and kingdom, and his fears over Christians aligning with the French or other rebellious forces fed his hostility.

Within a year of his ascension to the throne in 1847, his fear over the connection between Christianity and France brought his hostility toward the faith to a boiling point. He sought to cut off Vietnam from the rest of the world—and he issued a decree ordering all Christian missionaries to be killed by having a large stone fastened to their necks and their bodies thrown into the sea. The indigenous believers were not exempt from his animosity. Vietnamese church leaders and other believers were to be arrested, interrogated, and forced to renounce their faith. If they did not, the words "*ta do*" ("perverse religion") were to be burned into their cheeks to mark their "heresy." They would also be exiled into remote regions where they would stand little chance of survival. In 1851, Tu Duc issued a decree echoing the same orders, but adding that those found aiding or harboring Christians, either foreign or indigenous, were to be put to death—their bodies cut in two and thrown into the sea.

When in 1855 a revolt was led against the Nguyen dynasty by the rival clan, Tu Duc accused Christians of being involved in the rebellion. The accusations fanned the flames of his anger, leading him to issue a decree calling for the public decapitation of all Christians. The heads of those caught and killed were to be displayed in the streets for three days, to warn others of the consequences of following this "perverse religion." The homes of the victims were to be burned. Throughout the country, Christians were forbidden to gather together.

Six years later, still reeling from constant rebellions against his authority, from both internal strife and foreign aggressors, Tu Duc issued another anti-Christian edict in an attempt to root out the faith by scattering any remaining Christian communities. All Christians not imprisoned— from missionaries who had managed to survive to native believers—were to be dispossessed of their land and dispersed to non-Christian villages. For every one Christian in a village, five non-Christians were to be in place to monitor the village. Along with bearing the marks "*ta do*" on one cheek, Christians had the name of their village branded into the other, to increase the ability to monitor them. Families were separated, church communities broken, and communications between leaders and missionaries severed.

Tu Duc's treatment of Christians only further fueled France's quest to overthrow the nation and bring an end to the injustice and violence being unleashed in Vietnam.

In 1862, rebellions broke out as the French advanced, and Tu Duc feared his authority was crumbling. He believed the rebels would kill him, and so chose to make a deal with the French, reasoning that they would at least let him live—even if enforcing changes to his country and limiting his power. So he chose to sign the Saigon Treaty, giving away the southernmost portion of Vietnam, the Cochinchina region, to be a French colony and accepted the status of a French protectorate for his country. As a result of this treaty, he declared amnesty for scores of Christian prisoners—women, older men, and non-officials could be released whether or not they renounced their faith. Officials and young men who refused to renounce their faith, however, were to remain detained. Lands that had been confiscated (not burned) were also returned to their Christian owners.

As the French advanced on Vietnam, moving toward occupation, Tu Duc bowed to the pressure of their presence. On March 1871, the French ordered Tu Duc to renew his decrees of toleration toward Christianity which had begun his reign. The total number of Christians who lost their lives during the reign of Tu Duc is staggering—at least thirty thousand believers including twenty-five missionaries and three hundred church leaders.

Yet the French's presence during Tu Duc's reign also kindled fresh violence by nationalist sympathizers, specifically among the Van Than—staunch Confucianists who blamed the French occupation on followers of Christianity. Between 1873 and 1888, armed members of the group rampaged throughout Christian communities, setting fire to villages and killing thousands of Christians—most of them leaders.

After the death of Tu Duc in 1883, such bloody, fiery campaigns continued. A Nguyen king, Ham Nghi, launched a movement called "save the king," during which he asked the people to rally to him and resist the French. He also ordered the extermination of all Christians. Violence raged throughout Ham Nghi's reign, until he was arrested by the French army in 1886 and exiled to Algeria in 1888. Shortly thereafter, the Van Than movement was terminated, and Emperor Dong Khanh, the newly enthroned leader, officially reestablished freedom of religion in Vietnam.

Times of Death, Times of Growth

The nineteenth century was a time of persecution and death for Vietnamese Christians, but also a time of growth and victory. The church did not buckle under the brutality; in fact, even during the tribulations of Tu Duc's hostile reign, the church experienced great growth and laid the foundation for more flourishing and expansion. Despite the edicts and plots aimed and driving all Christians out of the country, some indeed survived—and managed to establish their own communities of faith. At the beginning of the twentieth century, there were 385 known church leaders ministering in the country, with an estimated total of 870,000 Christians by 1915.

In the coming years, the church would continue to multiply, carrying with it the paradox of persecution and expansion, death and growth, as it moved into a new chapter of obedient faith.

> *"Suffering is not the worst thing
> that can happen to us.
> Disobedience to God is the worst thing."*
>
> —A PERSECUTED VIETNAMESE CHRISTIAN

A CHURCH EMBATTLED
BY COMMUNISM
(1950s–1970s)

In the mid-twentieth century, communism took root in Vietnam and became one of the greatest sources of persecution the church would encounter.

Communism first gained power in Vietnam in 1930, when a Vietnamese Communist revolutionary leader founded the Indochinese Communist Party. From there he established the Communist-led Democratic Republic of Vietnam—formed in 1945, and further recognized by China and the USSR in 1950. With the fall of the French union in 1954, nations gathered for the Geneva Conference —a multinational conference with the purpose of finding a way to bring peace and unification to Indochina. The United States, the USSR, the United Kingdom, the People's Republic of China, and France were the main conference participants. Several countries also had limited participation— specifically, countries with some past involvement in the Korean War and First Indochina war. Documents to partition the country at the 17th parallel, dividing the North and South, were produced, called the Geneva Accord. The delegates from South Vietnam and the United States did not approve or sign the accord, but nonetheless it was passed.

The North and South partition was meant to be temporary, and for three hundred days civilians were free to travel across it. During that time, approximately one hundred thousand Christians fled from the North to the South, knowing persecution would come with the Communists.

For nearly two decades afterward, bitter civil war raged between North Vietnam and its communist allies and the government of South Vietnam, backed by anti-communist nations. Christ's people would be deemed "anti-country," "anti-government," and "unpatriotic" for refusing to deny their faith and embrace communism. Yet they would prove faithful to the Lord, who is over all authorities, governments, regions, and nations.

From the war's beginning on November 1, 1955, to its end in April 1975, the church most felt its chaotic affects in the North. Those who remained in the North faced immediate and sweeping harassment, from the confiscation of property to the destruction of Bibles and church buildings. All crosses on churches were reportedly removed from the buildings and many believers were imprisoned. There was also a comprehensive media propaganda campaign against Christians, painting them as unpatriotic troublemakers. As an attempt to squelch the spread of the gospel, the government placed strict controls on the activities of Christian leaders. Today, the Christian and Missionary Alliance, an organization that officially brought Christianity to Vietnam in 1911, is still not able to minister freely.

Christian Witness Amid Civil Strife

The efforts of the Communists certainly did slow the growth of the church through the long years of war. And yet, even in wartime, Vietnam proved to be a fertile ground for Christian witness, providing believers with unique opportunities to share Christ.

With the restrictions in the North, most of the mission organizations after 1954 were established in the South. The majority of Christian evangelism efforts were focused on the ethnic people in the Central Highlands, including the Montagnard and Hmong people. There was also considerable mission growth among the military forces.

To meet the needs created by the climate of war, both the Christian and Missionary Alliance and the Evangelical Church of Vietnam—two Protestant denominations—expanded their ministries to include a wider range of social, medical, and educational services. The need for emergency relief also led to a flood of new missions in the nation from other countries. The majority of the financial resources and missionaries came from the United States, but the work was not without its cost. At least eleven missionaries reportedly died at the hands of the Communists during the 1960s. And as the war raged on, there would be more losses to come.

A War Over, a Communist Takeover

In the 1970s, the decades of civil war came to an end, but persecution against the church continued. Even with a war over, communism's oppressive grip held strong. Yet even in a land riddled with post-war economic instability and ruled with an iron fist, Christ's faithful remained.

A peace treaty signed in 1973 led the United States to agree to withdraw its armed forces. North Vietnam's victory over the South in 1975 signaled the war's official end, as South Vietnam fell to Communist power. South Vietnamese President Nguyen Van Thieu resigned his power to Vice President Tran Van Huong, leaving the South with virtually no leader—and completely vulnerable to Communist rule. The takeover had begun.

As the Communists took control, they saw Vietnamese Christians as "foreigners"—countrymen dangerously connected to the West. Pastors and Christian leaders were frequent targets for violence by the government. All foreign missionaries were expelled and at least one hundred church buildings were forcibly closed. Almost one hundred pastors were sent to "reeducation" camps. Authorities regularly harassed believers, calling them to gather where they could be cursed and mocked and ordered to sign a paper denouncing their faith. American evangelist Billy Graham, fearing for the lives of Vietnam's Christian population in light of the increased persecution, attempted to evacuate several hundred Christians from a church building in Saigon. Unfortunately, his efforts failed, and the believers had to remain in the country. The execution of three pastors in 1978 proved that concerns for the lives of Vietnamese believers were indeed well-founded.

Such pressures inevitably drove some believers underground. Some would go to work for the Communist government, serving as teachers or in other roles.

Despite enduring intense persecution and years of strife, the church was not extinguished during the country's long civil war. Believers continued to live out their faith and reach out to others with the Good News. The courage and dedication of Vietnamese Christians continues to this day, a testament to God's enduring presence among the Vietnamese people, which would continue in the post-war years and beyond.

"BY FAITH, I CAN LIVE ON HOPE":
A MODERN-DAY TESTIMONY

Ethnic pastors and Christians are sometimes jailed for sharing the gospel in Vietnam. Following is a letter of gratitude from "Mary," a Vietnamese woman whose husband was imprisoned because of his faith in 2001. With help from VOM, she was able to visit him in prison.

"I thank God and thank you ... who have prayed for my family and helped me a lot with finances. Thank God, this time I can visit my husband for an hour. I was shocked to see my husband going to the visiting room; he was so weak, very pale and skinny. He could not walk by himself. He got a stomach ache because of the unclean food he eats every day. He often feels a headache because of the heavy beating from the police who tortured him savagely, making his lungs now weak.

"So I ask you, please don't forget to pray for my husband to be healed. By faith, I can live on hope; if not, I would be in depression. I thank God with all my heart and give thanks to you who have helped me wholeheartedly. Please continue to remember my husband, my children, and myself. May the Lord bless you."

DARING TO BUILD:
THE CU HAT CHURCH
(21ST CENTURY)

The attack was caught on cellphone video. If you watch it, you will see the thirty-three transport trucks storm onto the scene, right into the lush Central Highlands in Vietnam where one congregation had constructed their church building. In less than two hours, there would be nothing left of the structure but broken shingles on the trampled, tire-marked earth.

A Long Struggle

Nearly a decade ago, this congregation of more than five hundred Hmong Christians joined thousands of other Christians fleeing persecution in Vietnam's northwest provinces for the highlands. They did not start out with a church building of their own, but gathered to worship Christ in the home of one of the members, Mr. Di. But the small space was not suitable for corporate worship. Filled with the family's items, it made for crowded and crammed services. Many members would be forced to stand outside and participate from there, the blazing sun or torrential rains beating down on their bodies.

With concern for young mothers and children as the rainy season was approaching, the Christians of Cu Hat earnestly desired to build a chapel that had enough room for their whole congregation to worship under proper shelter. So they notified local authorities of their aspiration. They were told, however, that they would never get permission—that it would be useless to even ask, because an application to build a chapel would be considered only when the Tin Lanh ("Good News") Church of Vietnam was granted legal recognition. (See page 55 for more information on the "Good News" Church.) Again and again, members of their group had submitted registration applications, but government officials had simply ignored them.

In September 2008, after a long struggle, the Cu Hat Christians began to raise funds, determined to proceed because of their urgent need. They sent work teams into the forest to cut wood and saw lumber. They purchased red tile for the roof and brought it to the site. They hired some skilled workers and set about to construct a 12-meter by 20-meter (40-foot by 65-foot) chapel in front of Mr. Di's house.

But before all the walls were even completed, officials discovered their efforts and ordered them to stop. They commanded Mr. Di to cease building and to tear down what had already been con-

Members of the Cu Hat congregation building their church.

structed, on the charge that the lumber had been cut illegally.

The Cu Hat congregation met, prayed, and decided that they could not comply. Although virtually all buildings in this area of Vietnam are constructed without building permits, local authorities accused the Christians of "illegal construction" and ordered the congregation to "voluntarily" tear it down. On December 2, the district officials made a formal decision to demolish the church within two weeks if the Christians would not do so themselves.

The Day of Attack
The officials, police, and demolition workers arrived in vehicles with their license plates concealed.

Many others came on motorbikes. All were wearing civilian clothes and helmets. Some carried sticks, axes, or guns.

The group tried to force Mr. Di to sign a paper agreeing to the church building's demolition. They even grabbed his hand and tried to force his finger onto an ink pad and then onto a document, but he resisted too strongly. He eventually escaped into his house, where he fell onto his bed and buried his face in the covers. He could not bear to watch what was about to happen.

And with that, the mob began to demolish the chapel. Where hymns had been sung, chainsaws now buzzed and sledgehammers pounded. Wielding electric cattle prods, police beat back hundreds of distraught Christians who rushed to

The completed Cu Hat church building.

the site to protect the building. Some forty Christians ran into the chapel to pray. The government cadre ordered them to leave but they refused. An officer grabbed the arms of one of the believers and twisted them behind his back. Four others beat him with sticks. When he collapsed they dragged him out of the building and dumped him on the ground.

As additional violence broke out, several believers were tasered, some to the point of unconsciousness. At least four of them were women. Among the injured were a child who suffered a broken arm and a pregnant woman who fainted after being jabbed in the stomach with a cattle prod. Many others were interrogated about their religious activities on site or were taken to the police station.

After the mob confiscated the lumber, loading it onto their trucks, they emptied sacks of rice belonging to the church members onto the ground, put the roof tile into the sacks and sped away. The destruction was complete. It had taken a mere ninety minutes.

A Daring Determination

The repression of the officials was bold—shocking. But so was the endurance of the Cu Hat congregation. They refused to have their dedication to Christ broken.

One of the officials responsible for the attack remarked, "We destroyed it because it was a house of prayer." His words belie the foolishness of all those who seek to tear down Christ's Body with manmade weapons and machines.

That Christmas, just weeks after the attack, the Cu Hat Christians dared to build a temporary shelter of bamboo and tin to have a place to worship. There, in their makeshift meeting place, they celebrated the birth of the Savior who would, like them, be struck down, but not destroyed. There they gathered, giving praise to the Lord whose kingdom lasts forever.

CHRIST AMONG THE HMONG PEOPLE OF VIETNAM (20TH-21ST CENTURIES)

Over fifty ethnic minorities call Vietnam home, and the diversity of these people groups is staggering. They have come from different countries. They each speak their own language. Even the colors of their dress vary. Yet those among them who profess Christianity are united in this: they have been targeted by Vietnam's Communist regime.

In recent years, the persecution of Vietnam's Christians among ethnic minorities has been so intense that many of them have been driven out —not only from their homes, but from their country. Even those who flee to neighboring Cambodia aren't free from the long arm of Communist Vietnam, as Cambodian authorities, under an agreement with the Vietnamese government, often return the refugees to collect a bounty. Those who are returned are imprisoned, tortured, or killed.

Among the Hmong
Spread across the highland areas of Vietnam, near the Chinese border down to the 18th parallel, live the Hmong people. They are known for their artistry in embroidery—for their bright and elabo-

rately decorated clothes, and their "story cloths," which are woven pictures of recent Hmong history. Those in this tribe who have come to Christ have special stories of hardship threaded into their history: their lands taken from them, their churches torn down, their bodies beaten, and their family members imprisoned.

The Hmong people have been in Vietnam since the nineteenth century, when they emigrated from southern China in search of suitable farmland. They settled in the highland regions, building houses right into the mountains. The high altitude of their homes has kept them quite independent from other tribes and forced them into periods of considerable poverty, as the crops are sometimes difficult to harvest on the rocky slopes. Life has not been easy for this ethnic group.

Missionaries began reaching out to the Hmong people in the early twentieth century and built churches in the region. Animism—the belief that non-human entities, from animals to plants, are spiritual beings—was the driving spiritual force among the Hmong for centuries, and still is today. Traditionally, each home has an altar where people ask the various spirits for protection and mercy.

To abandon the animistic ways practiced for so many generations is to risk certain opposition. Communist authorities so fear the spread of Christianity—which they believe threatens their control

—that they encourage the Hmong to return to worshiping false spirits. During the Vietnam War between the U.S. and Communist forces, many Hmong sided with the U.S. troops and therefore were more intensely targeted for their stand against the regime.

But those who know the power of the Holy Spirit are not shaken by the pressure, or the fear of what traditions or spirits are lost when God is gained. When one Hmong Christian saw a fellow tribe member and his family wavering in the path to Christ, he told them, "If you trust Jesus, you will not lose your buffalo, pig, or chicken for the ghosts, but your spirit will be with Jesus in heaven." Shortly afterward, the man and his family came to Christ.

Hmong converts to Christianity have a long history of persecution.

After receiving many years of ministry from various denominations, approximately 50 percent of the Hmong population have now come to faith in Christ—at least three hundred thousand estimated in recent years. Most live in northern Vietnam where only about a dozen church buildings are officially allowed to exist.

Many sources reveal that the persecution of Hmong Christians in Vietnam has intensified in the last few years. Thousands of Hmong in North Vietnam continue to lose all for Jesus and are burned out of their villages. Some have been imprisoned and even killed. But Hmong Christians do not let such violence stop their ministry. They continue to go into the jungle and preach Christ, carrying the Word of God as their shield.

The bright witness of the Hmong people amid suffering can be heard in the words of Brother Musa So, who has been imprisoned for his faith since 2006. When police try to entice him to deny his Savior to secure freedom, he tells them, "We must obey God rather than men. When Hmong people trust the Lord, they never deny Him."

THE "GOOD NEWS" CHURCH OF VIETNAM

The Tin Lanh ("Good News") Church of Vietnam is the oldest indigenous Protestant group in the country. Its roots can be traced back to 1911, when a team of three international workers belonging to the Christian and Missionary Alliance (CMA) entered Da Nang (then considered part of Indochina). They purchased some land and set to work.

Robert Jaffray, a Canadian pastor, was the leader of this missionary team. Pastor Jaffray had long had a passion to touch the unreached in Southeast Asia with the gospel, and spent years as a CMA missionary in South China. The dedication and knowledge of this leader, teacher, and missions pioneer were indispensable in the founding and development of the Tin Lanh Church.

By 1927, the Tin Lanh Church had over four thousand members. The years that followed also contained tremendous growth. One hundred self-sufficient churches were in fruitful operation by 1940!

But the Tin Lanh Church was not without its periods of great challenge. During the Communist influence and infiltration of the 1960s, the government seized its Bible school and seminary, preventing crucial ministry training. After the Communist takeover in 1975, Tin Lanh members were among the many Vietnamese Christians to face violence for their allegiance to Christ.

Such suffering could have caused the Tin Lanh Church to crumble and the good news to be silenced. Yet it did not. Instead, the power of this church's witness has only grown stronger. By sacrificing their lives, working together in unity, and trusting God, this church has persisted and even expanded.

In 2001, the Tin Lanh group was registered with the government, granting it official legal recognition. Ten years later, in 2011, the Christian and Missionary Alliance and Tin Lanh Church held two days of special services and activities to commemorate one hundred years of ministry. Approximately fifteen thousand attended a celebration event in Da Nang's large indoor stadium. A CMA spokesman described this event as "marked by a great spirit of joy, a great spirit of gratitude to God because over those years the church had grown and developed to more than one million believers."

Today, the "Good News" Church continues to be a vibrant fellowship of indigenous Vietnamese Christians. Members are making an impact for Christ across the nation through home churches, orphanages, and volunteer outreach efforts.

Remember these devoted brothers and sisters in prayer as they carry on the tradition of faithful Christian witness and meet new challenges in their quest to bring God's truth and love to the people of Vietnam.

CHRIST AMONG THE MONTAGNARD PEOPLE OF VIETNAM (20TH-21ST CENTURIES)

In the Central Highlands of Vietnam lives an indigenous people called the Montagnards—the French term for "people of the mountains." It is a term that includes several specific ethnic peoples with distinct cultures and customs.

With their dark bronze complexions and lack of skin fold in the upper eyelid, these highland peoples are markedly different from mainstream Vietnamese in appearance. Their style of dress, cultural customs, and livelihoods also differ from those of their sister tribes. However, they, too, have endured violence, displacement, and harassment—particularly those who have dared to forsake traditional animist beliefs for Christianity.

The Montagnards in Vietnam were introduced to Christ in the 1850s by French Catholic missionaries. Some Montagnards embraced Catholicism, incorporating aspects of animism into their system of worship. By the 1930s, American Protestant missionaries were also active in the highlands, with the Christian and Missionary Alliance playing an especially prominent role.

When North Vietnam gained victory in the Vietnam civil war in 1975, churches in the Montagnard area of the Central Highlands were forcibly closed. Many Montagnard people were imprisoned while others joined the underground resistance army aligned with the United States and South Vietnam in the war. By the 1990s, however, many Montagnards gave up their military struggle and sought faith in Christ—looking for peace and hope in a tumultuous and violent time.

The past decade has proven especially painful for Montagnard Christians, with waves of repression and injustice washing across the mountain lands they call home. Officials have launched massive crackdowns on churches and have tortured believers in an effort to force them to renounce Christ and pledge their loyalty to the Communist Party of Vietnam. Much of the aggression is a reaction to the formation, in 2000, of a Montagnard activist movement called "Dega Protestantism." This form of evangelical Christianity advocated increased political autonomy and protection of ancestral lands, and was unsanctioned by the government. The Vietnamese government has since painted Montagnard Christians as an illegitimate religious group—a guise for a political independence movement. It continues to accuse believers of "anti-government activities" and claims they have been "infected by American Protestant thought." Hundreds of Christians have been given long prison sentences for threatening "national solidarity" for their involvement in peaceful public protests and unregistered house churches. The repression has been carried out against both "Dega" believers and those who do not consider themselves part of the movement. No Montagnard, it seems, is safe from harassment.

Praise and Faith in the Mountains

This unrelenting repression against ethnic minorities has yielded much sorrow, but it has failed to crush their faithfulness or the movement of Christ's love and truth in these regions.

Despite police threats, Vietnamese believers still conduct church activities like baptisms, even if they must do them under the cover of darkness or in a barrel of water. New believers continue to come to faith; baptisms have been increasing for the last fifteen years among the ethnic groups. The Montagnard believers are not content to keep God's Word to themselves or to their own hostile zones, but cross borders with their gospel lamps. They travel by motorbikes and climb mountains, walking hundreds of miles with the message of the cross. Although recent reports indicate as few as fifteen legal church buildings in the north, house church movements among northern peoples have spread.

VOM workers once met with a Vietnamese pastor who has worked with ethnic Christians for many years. He works long hours, giving up time

In some regions of Vietnam, Christians gather to study God's Word by flashlight.

with his family to take up the task. When asked why he serves in this way, with these people in their plight, he said, "I am most encouraged by the Christian fight of the ethnic people and the excitement in their heart for the ministry...They really love what the Lord calls them to do, although it is difficult."

The praise and faith of Vietnam's ethnic minorities echoes across the mountain countryside. It rings out in other restricted nations as an example of perseverance amid persecution. And it resounds across the worldwide Church with each voiced raised on their behalf.

Will you share their story?

A COMPASSIONATE CAPTIVE: THE STORY OF BETTY OLSEN

Betty Olsen was just thirty years old when she arrived in war-torn Vietnam to serve as a nurse at the Ban Me Thuot Missionary Compound. It was the mid-1960s, an extremely dangerous time to be involved in missionary work in the country. Just three years earlier, the Viet Cong had kidnapped three American missionaries serving in a leprosy hospital. They were taken into the dense jungle and never heard from again.

Although born to missionary parents in Africa, Betty's early life certainly didn't follow the typical path of female missionaries of the day. From the age of eight, she spent most of her time away at school. During high school, nursing school,

and missionary college in the United States, she was classified as a rebellious and insecure student who had difficulty establishing close relationships. Few would have marked her for the mission field.

Betty's first foray into mission work in the

Betty Ann Olsen

early 1960s—a trip to Africa to work alongside her father and stepmother—was a disaster. Long-held resentments surfaced, and Betty was considered so hard to work with that she was asked to leave. Depressed and convinced that no missionary agency would accept her, Betty contemplated suicide. However, she began to meet with a youth counselor at the local church, who helped her reach a place of stability and hope.

In 1964, the Christian and Missionary Alliance sent Betty to the Ban Me Thuot leprosy compound in Vietnam. It was a dangerous assignment, given the earlier Viet Cong abduction. She wrote in her testimony, "Most of the people that I have told about going to Vietnam are greatly concerned, and I appreciate this; however, I am not concerned, and I am very much at peace. I know that I may never come back, but I know that I am in the center of the Lord's will and Vietnam is the place for me."

And deadly danger did come. In January 1968, Viet Cong raided the compound again. For three days, they attacked the hospital, killing six missionaries with machine gun fire. Betty and Hank Blood, a Wycliffe Bible translator, were taken captive while trying to drive an injured coworker to the hospital.

Betty was chained to Hank and another American, Mike Benge, who had been volunteering in

Vietnam as an agricultural aid worker. They were forced to walk twelve to fourteen hours a day through mountainous jungles to reach successive prison camps where they were put in cages and given only boiled manioc root (a starchy root) to eat. Of the three prisoners, only Mike Benge survived to tell the story of their horrific captivity.

Dengue fever, paralyzing bouts of dysentery, and skin sores afflicted the prisoners daily. After several months, their malnutrition had caused their hair to gray and their teeth to fall out.

Betty's sacrificial nature and steadfast spirit shone even in this dark time. She would give most of her meager rations to the newly captured Vietnamese prisoners. When Mike had meningitis, she coaxed him out of delirium to eat, saving his life.

Betty herself became weaker by the day, and the Viet Cong began to kick and drag her to keep her moving. Mike, trying to defend her, was beaten with rifle butts.

On February 1, 1969, this brave and faithful sister died, finally, of the agonizing abuse at the hands of the Viet Cong. But her example of long-suffering love lives on, manifesting the Christlike compassion to which those in Vietnam, and beyond, are called.

"She never showed any bitterness or resentment," said Mike Benge. "To the end she loved the ones who mistreated her."

SEASONS OF VIOLENCE AND HOPE (21ST CENTURY)

In much of the world, Christmas and Easter are times in which followers of Christ can safely gather in peace to celebrate their Lord and Savior, Jesus Christ. But in restricted nations, these holidays are often times of fear and danger for believers—when authorities clamp down on, and even make a violent example of, those who obey Christ above all. Several holiday seasons of the past decade have held such trials for Vietnamese believers, yet they have also revealed the resilient faith of the men and women who serve a risen Savior.

Christmas Crackdowns

Christians belonging to the Montagnard ethnic group in Vietnam's Central Highlands have seen great hostility at the hands of officials during the Christmas seasons of recent years.

Christmas 2005 was a violent one. In the weeks leading up to Christmas, police rounded up and arrested dozens of Montagnard Christians and detained them in various prisons. In the early morning hours of December 8, security forces entered several villages in the province of Gia Long. They handcuffed at least seven Christians, kicking and beating them with batons. The men eventually passed out from the blows, and were thrown onto a truck and arrested. The detentions continued in the following weeks, and in Gia Long province alone, over one hundred Montagnard Christians were arrested by Christmas Eve.

Christmas-season persecution is not restricted to the rural regions. In December 2010, in the capital city of Hanoi, hundreds of Christians arrived at the National Convention Center for a planned Christmas event to find the doors locked and police on the scene. The officers tried to send them away, but the believers did not give in—in fact, they began to sing and pray in the square in front of the center. Police met their praise with aggression, striking at the Christians with their fists and nightsticks. The believers' bold act of worshiping the Messiah in the face of brutality, however, would not be forgotten. Theirs is another story to be added to the legacy of believers determined to obey God at all costs, regardless of man's attempts to shut them down.

Days of Persevering Faith

Easter celebrations and services have also been occasions of severe opposition for Vietnamese Christians, occasions when they have truly embraced the fellowship of their Savior's sufferings—some at the cost of their very lives.

Such was the price several believers paid in April 2004, when thousands of security forces attacked a gathering of Montagnard Christians in the Central Highlands. Thousands of believers were present, praying and peacefully speaking out against the government's suppression of Christianity, when the authorities launched their assault. Believers were beaten with electric cattle prods, battered with rocks, and shot. Scores were reportedly killed, and there were even reports of decapitations. The government attempted to paint their aggression as a necessary move to quell the ethnic group's quest for independence—but clearly more than just ethnic or land-rights issues were at the core of the gruesome assault.

Throughout Vietnam it is dangerous for Christians to gather for worship.

The president of the Montagnard Foundation, an organization created to preserve the Montagnard people, was sure to make plain the religious nature of the Easter massacre, saying, "All we want is to live as indigenous peoples on our ancestral lands without fear of persecution, without the Vietnamese authorities interfering in our religious affairs nor forcing us to renounce Christ, and without the fear our ancestral lands will be confiscated where we are driven to a life of poverty."

Though believers have not faced another attack the magnitude of the 2004 Easter massacre, the interference and opposition have continued, with Easter still proving to be a favored time for the government to wield its power unjustly against Christ's people. In April 2011, authorities in Vietnam prevented much-anticipated public Easter celebrations in Hanoi, despite having verbally promised organizers that the events could proceed. While the Christians were disappointed, they were far from surprised by the Communist government's action. "The authorities have clearly demonstrated to the world what we experience regularly—that their promises, whether verbal or written, cannot be trusted," said one church leader involved.

But that Easter was a paradox of disappointment and encouragement, of loss and of gain. The Christians shared, with great joy, that their efforts to stage the event had involved unprecedented cooperation among various Christian groups, from large house church groups to smaller fellowships. All emerged from the event more united in their efforts to stand firm amid government manipulation and pressure. Trust in the Lord prevailed, proving that His power will not be halted, nor His children hindered by earthly action and authority.

Songs of Praise
Not every Christmas or Easter has yielded abusive treatment of Christians by the government. There are moments when religious freedom has been recognized.

During Christmas 2009, some forty thousand people gathered in Ho Chi Minh City (Saigon) to worship God, celebrate the birth of the Savior, and hear a gospel message. Many believers were reportedly overwhelmed with emotion and gratitude, spontaneously hugging each other and crying out, "Lord, bring revival to all of Vietnam!" and "Nothing can stop the hand of the Lord!" Then on December 20, an estimated twelve thousand people attended a Christmas rally in Hanoi. Local sources said long-requested written permission for the event was never received, despite several reminders to authorities. However, four days before the event was to take place, Hanoi authorities and police told organizers that they would not interfere with the proceedings. "The sound of crying, of praise, of prayer were blended as one, beseeching Almighty God for spiritual revival in Vietnam," said a believer who attended the special gathering.

Similar songs of praise had rung out on Easter of that year, too. In April 2009, government officials granted atypical permission to unregistered house church groups to hold a public Easter service of more than fifteen thousand people at Tao Dan Stadium in Ho Chi Minh City. Many had been looking forward to the rare opportunity for large-scale fellowship, as they were accustomed to meeting in small groups. Though officials later demanded that the worship service be canceled, three hours before the evening service was scheduled to begin, officials relented and said it could proceed as planned. Just as the decision was announced, an unseasonal rain stopped, making the conditions for the stadium gathering much more favorable. The crowd sang with joy at the wondrous providence of their risen Lord as they gathered together to praise His name.

Crying, praise, and prayer—these are the faith-inspiring choruses that echo through the Vietnamese church's history of celebrating Easter and Christmas in their country. They resound in times of permission, peace, and calm; they ring out amid persecution and oppression. These are the "hymns" of believers with persevering faith—those who know that they do not need permission to worship God and proclaim the gospel even in seasons of affliction. In them is the sacrificial love of cross-bearing discipleship, the grace of a Savior who was born and died to give life, the anticipation of the day when all of the faithful will know only songs of eternal celebration.

THE PENALTY
FOR PROTESTING

By VOM-Australia

In Vietnam's major cities, there has been a huge swing by the newly educated generation to make a stand for religious freedom because they know it is supposedly guaranteed in the country's constitution. However, the government closely monitors religious activities and if they believe an activity undermines the country's peace, independence, and unity, and negatively affects the cultural traditions of the nation, it is considered illegal and must therefore be suspended. The government is paying particular attention to protests for religious freedom.

Recently there have been large demonstrations, especially in the north, by various groups who want their religious freedom. However, the authorities view this as anti-government and are using these rallies to eliminate all the "troublemakers" by severely beating the protesters. In many cases, they are arresting believers and placing them in prison for their actions. They often use excessive force against innocent protesters, and as a result, many have died from their injuries. The authorities also photograph the protesters for evidence, and VOM has met believers who have been imprisoned for six months, sometimes longer, after the protest occurred. One believer VOM interviewed was given a seven-year sentence in jail.

The persecution does not stop there, and the consequences of participating in protests affect many innocent people, including children. At a believer's home village, the authorities instill fear and intimidation in the other villagers, warning them not to support the spouse and children of the person arrested, or they, too, will face severe penalties. The authorities also place spies in the villages to report any suspicious activity. VOM heard firsthand of one such situation where a church elder was arrested for protesting. Fortunately, his wife was able to receive support secretly.

In this situation, the husband and wife had discussed the consequences they would have to face for being involved in the protest. They both knew the price they may need to pay because of his actions—including the possibility of imprisonment—and she agreed to support him no matter the cost. Normally the standard sentence is two years, but in this case it cost them dearly: her husband was sentenced to ten years! Nonetheless, they had agreed wholeheartedly that, regardless of what it cost them, they wanted the freedom to worship the Lord.

LAWS OF MAN, LAWS OF GOD (20TH–21ST CENTURIES)

For at least twenty years, Reverend Nguyen Hong Quang has been despised by Vietnam's Communist government for his knowledge of the law. Yet it is not ultimately Pastor Quang's knowledge of the laws of man for which he suffers; it is his steadfast dedication to the law of the Lord.

Pastor Quang has been repeatedly arrested and imprisoned, slandered in newspapers, and followed by police. A trained lawyer, he has intimate knowledge and understanding of how the regulations and legislations are used—and misused—in his country. He has challenged the government repeatedly on its violations of religious freedom, speaking out not just for himself but also for fellow believers facing church demolitions, torturous intimidation tactics, and other heinous acts against their faith.

When in 2004 the U.S. State Department designated Vietnam as a "Country of Particular Concern" for its violations of religious freedom, many were hopeful that the cycle of persecution against minorities might cease.

Following the international pressure, new legislation called the "Ordinance on Belief and Religion" came into force. The government also allowed the expansion of charitable activities by religious organizations. The following year, Vietnam signed an agreement with the U.S. government on religious freedom. It appeared the government was taking measures to halt the large-scale programs aimed at stopping the expansion of Christianity. A number of religious prisoners were freed, new congregations and house churches were registered throughout the country, and denominations were registered at a national level. In addition, the printing of Bibles was authorized in three ethnic minority languages of the Central Highlands—the first time since the Communist victory of 1975.

Pastor Quang

Religion, it seemed, was able to be practiced more freely in Vietnam.

But with these new freedoms came the reminder that legislation alone could not stop the government from abusing their authority against those they considered "enemies of the state." The laws can still be bent and used by authorities to control and limit Christian activity. According to the *Ordinance on Beliefs and Religions*, local officials are required to "carefully examine if there is a need for religious belief" before granting registration to a church. The government therefore delays or outright denies churches as it pleases, if it deems them "unnecessary" or "subversive," or determines that they "negatively affect the unity of the people or the nation's fine cultural traditions."

The road to registration is a risky one, fraught with resistance and duplicity from Vietnam's ruling officials. The very act of submitting a registration application for a church or Christian organization can trigger government abuse. Christian groups have been harassed—their services stopped or members beaten—immediately after submitting their registration applications. Almost no churches in villages have received approval, while some churches in major cities have been approved.

As a rule, application procedures are confusing and contradictory, and the process is lengthy, requiring several legal stages. Religious organizations, for example, begin the process by applying for registration in each local administrative area of operation. They also have to submit detailed information to authorities that outlines the leadership, structure, and activities of their organization. Vietnam's Governmental Committee for Religious Affairs (CRA) must then also issue the organization a license in order for them to receive official registration. Overall, it is a long and detailed process ripe for potential setbacks, should the government wish to delay or prevent the process from reaching completion.

The only registered, and therefore legally recognized, Protestant churches in Vietnam are the Evangelical Church of North Vietnam and the Evangelical Church of South Vietnam. Even these denominations, however, are under constant watch. Vietnam's Assemblies of God Church (AoG, an international group of 140 autonomous but associated Pentecostal churches) worked toward registration. A key advancement occurred in October 2011, when the Assemblies of God Church in Vietnam received an "operating license" giving the congregations permission to carry on religious activity throughout the country for one year. The AoG Church was also preparing a doctrinal statement, a constitution and bylaws, and a four-year working plan in accordance with the license. In order for them to hold an organized assembly, these documents and plans would then need to be approved by the government. In a December 2011 Compass Direct report, one source referred to the AoG as "newly registered." When dealing with a government that has a proven track record of unreliability and deceit, it is understandable that even those encouraged by this license might look upon the future with a wary, cautious hope.

The Registration Question

There is no guarantee that registration will safeguard Christians from being hassled by the government or from other forms of persecution. In some cases, Christian groups that have chosen to register locally but not nationally are viewed with suspicion by authorities. The question is: is registration a step toward religious freedom, or simply a means for the government to tighten its grip on the actions and initiatives of churches?

Among believers there are mixed views on whether or not registration should be pursued. Pastor Quang's Mennonite congregation, for example, has yet to be registered and reportedly has no plans to. The pastor believes that government registration of churches is the new front-line in the battle for religious freedom in his country.

He says there is ample evidence that it would in no way stop the harassment that has followed him over the years.

"Registration is not freedom of religion," Pastor Quang shared. "If we want to organize a Christmas celebration, we have to ask for permission. If we have a pastor ordination, we have to ask permission. Registration is like giving our hand into tighter control."

To register or not to register—it appears that any course a Christian group takes can place it in a potential line of fire. As such, it is a decision to be considered prayerfully, and a dilemma that should not be diminished by those seeking to understand the challenges facing Vietnamese believers advancing God's kingdom today.

Persistent Persecution

The government of Vietnam made a very public effort to be removed from the U.S. State Department's list of countries of concern and was successful in 2006. But against this apparent progress are incidents that prove there is still good reason to be concerned for followers of Christ in the nation. The saga of persistent harassment against Pastor Quang and his congregation is unmistakable proof of the government's ongoing desire to quash all those with a love for and loyalty to Christ.

The destruction of church buildings is another tactic used often to intimidate believers and hinder their public worship—especially those of well-known Christian leaders and large congregations. In December 2010, an estimated five hundred soldiers and police demolished a two-story building that was both the home of Pastor Quang and the headquarters of the Vietnam Mennonite church. He was beaten unconscious when he objected to the arrest of twenty Bible school students.

Other Christian advocates who speak up for the persecuted minorities have also suffered greatly in recent years. In 2007, two prominent lawyers, Nguyen Van Dai and Le Thi Cong Nhan, were sentenced to four and five years in prison, respectively, followed by four-year and three-year periods of house arrest, for "disseminating slanderous and libelous information against the Socialist Republic of Vietnam." In 2011, Nguyen Van Dai was released after serving his sentence, and must fulfill a four-year administrative, or house arrest, sentence. In 2011, after a closed-door trial, Vietnam officials sentenced land-rights campaigners and democracy activists to up to eight years in prison for "subversion"—allegedly for affiliating with a banned opposition group and an unsanctioned Christian house church.

In the face of deceptive setbacks in religious freedom and outright injustice, these experts in the law and countless other Vietnamese Christians press on with the strength of Christ. They speak up and stand up for their faith, knowing Who holds true authority.

"The Communists here use politics to control the people, because when the people know the Lord, there is no more fear," said one Vietnamese evangelist. "They are no longer under bondage when they become the children of God. Christians live under the Bible's law."

Such words reveal the current of obedience running through the Vietnamese Christian community—their faith is constant, relentless, liberating. Vietnam's laws may change, churches may or may not seek registration, but through it all the faithful press on.

PRAYERS OF
HIS PEOPLE

*"Sometimes Christians pray for more
guidance before they testify for the Lord.
We want God to send us a letter telling us
what will happen when we obey Him.
We want God to take out all of the risk.
But, we know the way to God. We do not
need guidance. The apostles prayed for
boldness to speak the Word of God, not if
they should speak. We need courage and
faith. We need to go forward."*

—HMONG CHRISTIAN

*"Prayer was the best food that
kept me strong."*

—A FORMERLY IMPRISONED VIETNAMESE PASTOR

*"The church [in Vietnam] is now on stormy
seas but the boat still goes out. The Lord
enables us to row together. Be at peace.
I ask you and the Church to pray for us."*

—PASTOR NGUYEN HONG QUANG

THUGS, THREATS, AND BRIBES: NEW STRATEGIES FOR OPPRESSION

By Riley K. Smith with VOM-Australia

Requiring congregations to register with the government has been an oft-used excuse for authorities in Vietnam to oppress the church. Simply put: no registration, no church. The Love Baptist Church in Phu Quy Hamlet in the central province of Quang Nam experienced this in October 2011, when police barged into the church's worship service and demanded they stop worshiping God. When the pastor asked them to wait until the end of the service so he could speak with them, they refused and shut down the church's sound system. Despite submitting an application to the government twice to register, the church had been denied by the authorities both times.

Earlier, police had called a number of the church's members to the station. Perhaps the congregation's hopes were raised that registration would finally be approved. Instead, authorities yelled at the church members and tried to force them to sign a commitment not to worship God. If they refused to sign it, they would not be allowed to return home. Some were overcome with fear and signed it. However, the pastor received a different threat, one that appeared to tip the hand of the Vietnamese authorities regarding their new strategy to silence the church. They warned him, "If you continue to gather many people to worship God, and there is someone who comes to disturb you, we will not take responsibility. At that time, don't call us!"

Around 1:00 p.m., just two hours after the police barged into the church building ordering the service to stop, that threat became a reality.

About forty hired thugs bearing tattoos arrived at the congregation's place of worship. Some entered while others remained outside, but they clearly stated their purpose to the pastor's family members who were present: to find the pastor and eliminate him. They tried attacking the pastor's father, but he was able to defend himself. He cried out to Jesus and ordered them to leave. Soon, they fled on motorbikes but not before they threatened, "We will return and kill all of you. Let's see whether you can continue to worship or not!"

After the thugs fled, the pastor called the police and a Communist Party official, but no one answered his call. He was ignored, just as he had been warned.

When they heard what had happened, a number of believers went to the church building and prayed with the pastor. He assured them that he would be fine and sent them home. But it wasn't over.

At 8:30 that night, the pastor and his family awoke to the sound of glass breaking. He wanted to confront the thugs, but his wife refused to let him, as she knew what awaited him: certain death. Still, the thugs managed to find his whereabouts in the home and tried to break down the door with steel bars. When members of the pastor's family who were in another part of the house tried to stop the thugs, they were beaten. Hearing them cry out in pain was too much for the pastor and he wanted to rush to their aid, but his wife forbade him, telling him, "If you go, they will kill you immediately! Their target is you, not others." With his wife clearly frightened, all the pastor could do was cry out to the Lord for help. Calling the police was again futile, as no one answered his call.

All the while, he continued to hear sounds of his family members crying for help. No one in their neighborhood could help them because their home was surrounded. Finally, the thugs left. The pastor stepped outside and was devastated by the sight of his injured family. For a while, the pastor remained home, and many believers from the congregation gathered there to protect him and his family. "I am very proud to be a pastor of this courageous people!" he shared. "Thank God for giving me a father, a brother, and many brothers and sisters in the same belief who were willing to sacrifice their lives for me . . ."

Just one month later, Compass Direct reported that a gang of thugs attacked leaders of a Baptist house church near Hanoi, in northern Vietnam. Leaders of the church were gathered for a spiritual renewal meeting at the home of Pastor Nguyen Danh Chau, when the thugs interrupted them at 9:30 a.m. They beat the participants and damaged their property, including a pulpit used for church services in the home. They tore down the cross hanging on a wall and tossed it into a nearby body of water. Sources say this act alone exposes the thugs' motivation for the attack. They stole parts from four motorbikes belonging to the pastors before destroying them, leaving the bikes irreparable. They seriously injured over a dozen believers and warned Pastor Chau that they would kill him if he kept bringing Christians together.

During the attack, some of the thugs ran outside and announced that the Christians were beating up people inside. As the thugs had planned, a crowd soon gathered, which would prevent the Christians from fleeing the scene. Pastor Chau was beaten and lost consciousness for several hours, and all of the injured were later taken to the hospital. However, the denomination's leader was concerned that they would not be helped, as doctors in Vietnam are known to refuse treatment to patients when the violence is religiously motivated.

Ironically, these believers were attacked on the International Day of Prayer for the Persecuted Church (IDOP), November 13, 2011. The report of this incident notes that in light of official policy toward religion growing increasingly tolerant, police and other higher officials have made use of hired thugs to carry out attacks against Christians. Christian leaders have observed that legal action is rarely taken against these thugs, whose identities often remain unknown. However, occasionally their identities are known, especially those who attacked "Pastor Lanh."

In May 2011, police hired a drunkard in Pastor Lanh's village to beat and harass him. On one occasion the thug beat Pastor Lanh's father nearly to death as he was taking a fellow villager to the hospital for medical attention. Some of the other villagers came to his rescue; otherwise, he would have died. His father is now unable to work in the fields. The thug also threw stones at Pastor Lanh's roof, damaging it.

The thug was so enraged when his own mother turned to Christ that he beat her with a chair, bringing her life on this earth to an end. When villagers reported the murder, police said they would investigate, but they never did. At the funeral, the man held out a long knife and threatened to kill the one hundred believers present. Afraid that he would carry out his threats, they all left.

All that Pastor Lanh could do was report to the police that the thug had attacked his father as well as damaged his roof, but nothing was done. No arrest was made of the thug—not even for killing his own mother. He continued to lash out at Christians, and two months later he beat another Christian man and cracked his skull.

The reason Christians believe this thug works for the police is that even when officers arrest him they incarcerate him for only one day. Today he is back in the village.

Pastor Lanh fears for his life and told believers that one day he may be killed by the thug, who lives close to Lanh's house. Every time Pastor Lanh sees the drunkard, he runs in the opposite direction. Not knowing how to deal with him, Lanh requests prayer for this situation.

Bribes and Threats

Pastor Hong Quang Nguyen has witnessed various tactics being used against his students, as he and his Mennonite Bible School in Ho Chi Minh City have been targeted by government authorities. In December 2010, authorities destroyed both his home and his school, causing them to relocate. But that did not stop Pastor Quang from equipping students and evangelizing in the area. He firmly believes that the government is trying to destroy the Mennonite churches in central Vietnam. And if Christians like Pastor Quang remain undeterred after their homes and schools are destroyed, authorities will employ other means to silence the church, including bribery. Pastors and other Christians are frequently offered bribes, such as a house and a water buffalo, from the government if they will leave their Christian faith. Some accept; others do not.

Police tried to bribe students from two of Pastor Quang's classes to leave the school. Three students were offered a passport, 30 million Vietnamese *dong* (about four years' salary), and a job in Malaysia if they would leave the church and abandon their studies at the school. One student agreed to the offer; the other two refused it. In one of the classes, many of the students were offered positions as the chief of police in their home district or as the head of community organizations if they will leave Christianity. They all rejected the offer.

In 2011, authorities from Hanoi arrived in five luxury cars at Pastor Quang's school and took three students to lunch. While at lunch, the students were told that if they would kill Pastor Quang (by "accident" or other means), they would be given laptop computers, 100,000 Vietnamese *dong*, and the pastor's house. The students told Pastor Quang what the police had said. They thought the police were joking and could not believe that they would ask the students to kill him. When VOM asked Pastor Quang how he feels about such threats, he said this has been normal since he began his ministry. Even the treasurer of the Mennonite Church was offered a reward to leave the denomination.

These bribes are not confined to evangelical Christians. Catholics and Buddhists have also been approached by the government to leave their religious beliefs. Many have accepted the bribes.

Those who refuse to be bribed are persecuted by being denied all government support, including medical care, education, and assistance for farming. Graduates from Pastor Quang's school have experienced similar consequences. He shared, "The government cuts them off from all societal benefits. Poor Vietnamese normally get interest-free loans to buy necessities. These are withheld. Medical care is provided free of charge, but the graduates and their families are denied access. Seeds for planting crops are given each year by the government, but the graduates are not given them anymore. The government will also sometimes take away their water buffaloes so farming becomes much more difficult. The government officials say, 'You have a God, let Him help you.'"

Authorities are trying to divide the churches that are members of the Vietnam Evangelical Fellowship (VEF), which consists of twenty-nine church groups that have joined together. Some senior pastors have been offered a passport to go overseas if when they travel they will tell others that there is no persecution in Vietnam. One denominational leader accepted the offer and said there is no more persecution in Vietnam, even though he knows that many believers are currently being persecuted and have experienced severe beatings over the years.

Every two years the VEF votes for a new leader. Five minutes after the vote, the police call to congratulate him. This is their way of letting the believers know that they see "everything."

But so does the Lord. He is *El Roi*, the "God who sees" (Genesis 16:13). As Vietnamese Christian leaders face thugs, threats, and bribes, pray they rest in the eternal Judge who does not miss anything and will one day bring all to account.

NEW PATTERNS EMERGE AMONG PRISONERS

By VOM-Australia

Through many interviews with believers who have been imprisoned for their faith, VOM has found a pattern emerging among those who are about to be released from prison. Over a period of time, it appears that authorities are putting forms of untraceable chemicals into the prisoners' daily food. These chemicals affect their digestive organs, causing stomach ailments associated with food poisoning. Once the prisoners are released and have medical examinations, the doctors find they need treatment for many associated intestinal ailments.

A poor diet in prison is another major contributor to stomach problems. Released prisoners have related that the guards place sand in their rice or feed them the same grain that is fed to pigs and bullocks. The vegetables are grown in "gardens" of human waste—all designed to cause major health complications, even death.

VOM has also been told that prisoners are systematically injected with chemicals that make them violently ill. They experience lethargy, vomiting, and dehydration—a dangerous weakened state that requires careful medical attention. If not treated, they can die. Although the drug appears to be medically untraceable, VOM has received reports of this same method being used on prisoners in China.

CONCLUSION:
PERSEVERANCE,
PRAYER, PROMISE

Today, Vietnam remains one of the most tightly controlled nations in the world. Throughout the country—from the North, to the South, to the Central Highlands—authorities continue to launch attacks on house churches, destroying property and interrogating believers. In an alarming trend, Communist youths, fed the rhetoric of Christianity as a "false religion," have been incited to attack believers' homes and church buildings.

Horrific stories continue to surface of Christians, many new converts, being pressured by officials to recant their faith—either by threats of financial loss or by vicious beatings. How tempting it must be to bow to the pressure to avoid having your family become financially destitute or your body put through excruciating pain.

Perseverance

Why are the Communists—a Party with complete political power—so fearful of Christians, a minority? Why are the Christians' holiday celebrations and peaceful protests thwarted? To the outsider, they would seem harmless. But the truth is, Vietnamese Christians do have a "dangerous" faith. They stand in direct and bold opposition to the atheistic Communist government that has a stranglehold on their country. The believers persevere—they lose their lands, property, church buildings, and even their loved ones, yet they press on in faith.

And the church is not just enduring, but growing. The ethnic peoples of central and southern Vietnam have seen a ninefold increase in the number of Christians in the past thirty years, despite the heavy tide of persecution and trial. Registered or unregistered, in the city or in the mountains, congregations continue to meet, even though their members face routine interrogations and threats.

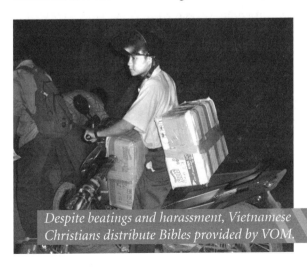

Despite beatings and harassment, Vietnamese Christians distribute Bibles provided by VOM.

Pastor Quang and his congregation are among those facing such pressures. Yet even with a history of persecution and a present full of hardships, Pastor Quang is confident in Christ. He and his congregation are determined to continue proclaiming their faith in the risen Lord, trusting Him and seeing through the bitter tactics of their oppressors.

"Once we serve God surely we must go the way of the cross, so I will not quarrel against the Lord for what has happened," Pastor Quang said. "Once the government tries to use violence it means they are defeated already."

Prayer

One former worker with VOM-USA vividly remembers a conversation he had about prayer with Vietnamese Christians he visited in the late 1990s. Knowing the long-standing political conflicts the Communist nation had suffered, he asked these believers if their prayer was for the country's borders to open up to the gospel, as they had in Eastern Europe. "No," they responded. "We pray that the heavens open up."

It was a response that we should never forget —an answer that testifies to how passionately these believers want to see others come into the kingdom, and one that helps the faithful worldwide know how to pray for those serving Christ in Vietnam.

Can you follow this example of prayer by lifting up your Vietnamese family? Pray that ethnic Christians will continue their witness "to obey God rather than men" (Acts 5:29). Pray for freedom for those imprisoned for their faith. Pray also for their families, that they may know the comfort of Christ and rest in His provision. Pray that God will work in the fearful hearts of the Communist leaders, bringing them to repentance and fellowship with Him.

Along with raising your voice to the Lord in prayer, you can raise a voice by picking up a pen and writing letters. You can get involved in helping to break down the barriers of isolation surrounding those serving Christ in prison or underground. You can write letters of encouragement to prisoners themselves by visiting The Voice of the Marytrs' letter-writing website at www.PrisonerAlert.com. You can also subscribe to *The Voice of the Martyrs* newsletter to stay informed of the testimonies and needs of the church in Vietnam and walk alongside them as they suffer.

Promise
God has not promised His children in Vietnam freedom from trials and oppression in this life.

He has not promised this for any of us, not here. It is a hard truth, but it is the truth. Yet even in the tightly controlled nation of Vietnam, He holds dominion and the promise of deliverance—not days of deliverance or even centuries, but for eternity. His love is unfailing and life-changing, allowing us to, like Betty Olsen, love those who mistreat us or, like Andrew of Phu Yen, cry out "Jesus!" in the face of death.

And so, as you remember your suffering family in Vietnam, pray that they, too, will continue to be emboldened and inspired to adopt the same posture of humble obedience taken by their Lord. And may their stories make your own steps light as you journey in the way of the cross.

Today, despite continuing persecution, Vietnamese are finding faith in Christ.

FOR FURTHER READING

The following sources, a selection of those consulted in the writing of this book, are recommended for further reading and research.

Gilley, Sheridan and Brian Stanley, eds. 2006. *Cambridge History of Christianity: Volume 8, World Christianities c. 1815–c. 1914.* New York: Cambridge University Press.

Marshall, Paul A. 2007. *Religious Freedom in the World.* Latham, MD: Rowman & Littlefield Publishers.

Phan, Peter C. 2006. *Mission and Catechesis: Alexandre de Rhodes and Inculturation in Seventeenth-Century Vietnam (Faith and Cultures).* Maryknoll, NY: Orbis Books.

Ramsay, Jacob. 2008. *Mandarins and Martyrs: The Church and the Nguyen Dynasty in Early Nineteenth-Century Vietnam.* Stanford, CA: Stanford University Press.

Shortland, John Rutherford. 1875. *The Persecutions of Annam, a History of Christianity in Cochin China and Tonking.* London: Burns and Oates.

Simonnet, Christopher. 1988. *Theophane Venard: A Martyr of Vietnam*. San Francisco: Ignatius Press.

White, Tom. 1996. *Between Two Tigers*. Bartlesville, OK: Living Sacrifice Book Company.

Online Resources

Compass Direct: www.compassdirect.org

Human Rights Watch: www.hrw.org

OMF-International Canada: www.omf.ca

The Voice of the Martyrs monthly newsletter and websites:

    www.persecution.com (USA)
    www.persecution.net (Canada)

RESOURCES

The Voice of the Martyrs has available many books, videos, brochures, and other products to help you learn more about the persecuted church. In the U.S., to request a resource catalog, order materials, or receive our free monthly newsletter, call (800) 747-0085 or write to:

The Voice of the Martyrs
P.O. Box 443
Bartlesville, OK 74005-0443
www.persecution.com
thevoice@vom-usa.org

If you are in Australia, Canada, New Zealand, South Africa, or the United Kingdom, contact:

Australia:
Voice of the Martyrs
P.O. Box 250
Lawson NSW 2783
Australia

Website: www.persecution.com.au
Email: thevoice@persecution.com.au

Canada:
Voice of the Martyrs, Inc.
P.O. Box 608
Streetsville, ON L5M 2C1
Canada

Website: www.persecution.net
Email: thevoice@vomcanada.org

New Zealand:

Voice of the Martyrs
P.O. Box 5482
Papanui, Christchurch 8542
New Zealand

Website: www.persecution.co.nz
Email: thevoice@persecution.co.nz

South Africa:

Christian Mission International
P.O. Box 7157
1417 Primrose Hill
South Africa

Email: cmi@icon.co.za

United Kingdom:

Release International
P.O. Box 54
Orpington BR5 9RT
United Kingdom

Website: www.releaseinternational.org
Email: info@releaseinternational.org

RESTRICTED NATIONS SERIES

Through the Restricted Nations series, learn about Christianity in the following countries, from the introduction of the gospel message until today, when Christians are persecuted for their faith. Weaving historical accounts with modern-day testimonies, these books will challenge you to share in the sufferings of Christians around the world and inspire you to pray for the persecuted Church today.

China

Colombia

Eritrea

India

Indonesia

Iran

North Korea

Pakistan

Sudan

To order these and other resources, visit www.VOMBooks.com

China:
*The Blood-
Stained Trail*
(ISBN 978-0-
88264-029-7)

Colombia:
*The Gospel Invades
Enemy Territory*
(ISBN 978-0-
88264-033-4)

Eritrea:
*A People
Imprisoned*
(ISBN 978-0-
88264-028-0)

India:
*Tales of
Glory*
(ISBN 978-0-
88264-032-7)

Indonesia:
*Called to
the Cross*
(ISBN 978-0-
88264-025-9)

Iran:
*Finding Hope in
the Axis of Evil*
(ISBN 978-0-
88264-031-0)

North Korea: *Good
News Reaches the
Hermit Kingdom*
(ISBN 978-0-
88264-030-3)

Pakistan:
*An Enduring
Witness*
(ISBN 978-0-
88264-034-1)

Sudan:
*Afflicted But
Not Forgotten*
(ISBN 978-0-
88264-026-6)

*To order these and other resources, visit
www.VOMBooks.com*